Dawn in Cities

By Gary Beck

Winter Goose
Publishing

Winter Goose Publishing
2701 Del Paso Road, 130-92
Sacramento, CA 95835

www.wintergoosepublishing.com
Contact Information: info@wintergoosepublishing.com

Dawn in Cities

COPYRIGHT © 2013 by Gary Beck
First Edition, February 2013
ISBN 978-0-9881845-9-6

Cover Art by Winter Goose Publishing
Typeset by Michelle Lovi

Published in the United States of America

Poems from *Dawn in Cities* have been published by: Alura, Blue Print Review, Bitterroot, Caravan, Decanto Poetry Magazine, Green's Magazine, Poem, Poetry Today, Portland Review, San Fernando Poetry Journal, Voices, Chantarelle's Notebook, The Innisfree Poetry Journal, Wolf Moon Press Journal, Istanbul Literary Review, Nashwaak Review, Poetry Monthly, The Persistent Mirage, Words on Paper, Contemporary Rhyme, Blue Fifth Review, Remark Poetry, Lucid Rhythms, Istanbul Literary Review, Written Word, Thick With Conviction, Munyori Poetry Journal, Rogue Poetry Review, Madswirl, Write Me A Metaphor, Starfish Poetry, Spokes, Concrete Meat Sheet, Publishing Genius, A Little Poetry, Sentinel Poetry Journal, RKVRY, Faraway Journal, Clearfield Review, Poet's Ink Review, Media Cake Magazine, Toronto Quarterly Review, The Commonline Project, Spark Bright Magazine, Ranfurly Review, Baltimore Is Reads, Farmhouse Magazine, The Ugly Tree, Pure Francis, and Foundling Review.

To N.G.
Nothing is constant
That is why we strive

Table of Contents

Decline

I left a town of wood and brick
and reached a tortured city,
heart of steel,
soul of glass.
I looked into your kindless face
and saw no pity,
just the frozen mask
that suffering never melts.

As hopes impaled themselves
on frigid pinnacles,
city, growing taller, colder,
distant to the outcasts of despair,
I heard wild dogs howling,
prowling desolate boulevards,
crying for departed masters
like abandoned children
shivering in vacant buildings,
comforted only by responsive rats.

And no voices were raised
as the city of abundance crumbled.
No demands, or pleas for endurance.
Only the relics of desertion whispered
the final moments of prosperity.

Untranquil

The roar of engines shocks the night,
wheels hum, whine, screech on darkling streets.
The clop of hooves, neighs, moo's, cockadoodle doo's
no longer prod our sleeping windows.
The million snarls of grumpy motors,
grumbling and complaining of the coming day,
throttle the grating voice of morning man
striving to command the dawn.
Recalcitrant machines resist
man's jostling for control of life.
The brief doze of the city is shattered.
The sounds of drive break the last peace.
The calm thought and quiet dream is forgotten.

Vigil

The brief night silence slowly fades.
The snorting wind runs home to nest.
The sleep of houses day invades
and pokes dulled dreamers from their rest.
The traffic sounds the hour to rise.
The light bulbs cruelly end the gloom.
The sleepy dust makes bleary eyes
blink at the odor in the room.
The morning yawns and curls its paws
'round men who rush to work in herds
with razor cuts upon their jaws,
they never hear the songs of birds.
Their cigarette and coffee through,
men start machines and in their fright
forget the sleepless poet who
in every city guards the night.

Conflict

Long night's tide
drifting shoreward.
Sea muse chanting
of the eternal dawn,
swifter than a cry of pain,
pounding madly,
a frightened schizophrenic on a prison door,
floating on the bitter fumes
of endless industrial nights,
rocking, rocking,
through the crime night streets of cities
furtively fading into doorways
when grim cadavers march like Caesar's legions.
All Gaul is divided . . .
Night, day, anguish . . .
Clashing barbarian host.

Outreach

Time is the dreary me, making
the hunger for people a citadel
far beyond storming; my weakness
building me a nothing empire,
powerless on a windswept globe.

Passing tenants on this unheeding earth
make mock of endless universe.
At dawn we'll promenade a moment
on tiny road through fragile city,
strutting our limitless power.

Our planet spins and circles
a curious pattern that we never see,
keeping us clinging, timid mites
barking our voices in darkness,
looking the bright star specks unknown.

Brief pause in man's mighty conception,
the sickly humiliation of fear
quickly forgotten in arrogant visions
that our few billion bits
will someday fill the universe.

Famished City

Night sounds soothe the city . . . Lost boat crying on a foggy river . . . The tick and tock of hungry time . . . Endeavors dreamed and forgotten. The distance of a thousand hopes not as far as sleep. People stirring in a great and frightened land. Boys of footballs and six-gun triumphs. Girls of proms and dolls. Men and women of briefcases and decisions. The sob and sigh of unfound promises, lost in the exhaust roars of trucks, cars, planes. The rumbles and rattles of awakening. A monster city crawls to life, devouring its tenants.

Careless Seed

Turn enchantment backwards
before tomorrow's birth,
or old men seated by imagined fires
will steal all visions.
Creaks and grumbles time
has never made objection
to, nothing, nohow,
so what are we waiting for.
We are mostly words and crimes,
instants of beauty.
Let us dare to say it . . . Beauty.
Moments will sometimes grow pauses
never, never long enough
to weep good tears.
So kick the old men from their places
and let the dark, cold nights of city streets
end each dawn when someone new
is betrayed into the world.

42nd Street Remembered

The dawn strands of 42nd Street fog
hulk and squat from west river sludge
to the eastern peepshow outpost,
twining tendrils of conceal,
mysteries of low appetite,
petty evil, gross and cruel,
displayed for those who seek
the beckoning of smut films
eager for lust-yearning patrons,
fellow citizens, peers, brothers,
responding to the bare allures of tease,
who pay, sate, go . . .
Nothing better know.

Indifference

The siren shrieks through city streets,
no one hurries fast enough.
The sound foretells
crime, fire, pain, death,
but no one hurries fast enough.
Overloaded circuits falter,
overburdened people doze.
The yell, the cry, the scream,
pierces the callous dawn,
mostly ignored,
one plea too many
in this relentless life.

Visions of New York City

The wind blows down chimneys,
an animal howl
serenading an old crone's dreams.
Tenements are stooped old men, faces sagging.
Ragpicker limping,
gunnysack full of treasure.
A thousand children
lie in rotting bananas,
they never saw the sun.
Santa comes on spider tendrils
afraid to stir the East Side soot.
Mrs. Lopez lifts her window,
Santa never visits her,
she always smells of wine.
A headless snowman sheds hot tears
that burn tiny holes in his chest.
Last scurry
and Christmas slinks off with speckled rats.

What is a final dream,
the last vision before panthers?
An old man plays an older fiddle,
gathering pennies.
In the summer,
naked and full of curses,
children open fire hydrants on the Lower East Side.

Captain Lewis, officer and gentleman,
runs the Salvation Army mission on the Bowery.
The bums listen to preaching
to get hot soup.
Hermano Lopez waits on line at the relief office.
The woman with the moustache is there today.
She always asks why he can't speak English.
He would spit on her, but his family would starve.

After the novena the worshippers have a festival
on narrow streets lined with enticements.
Girls are pinched from booth to booth.
Four Italians beat up a Puerto Rican.
A drunk is dragged into a doorway and robbed.
Everyone loses money at the games of chance,
the saint has blessed the wheel.
The evening gets tired
and decides to go home.
A good time was had by some.

Barren Land

O makers of cities
in your threadbare revelation,
coursing crumbling streets
that cry hunger like wares,
your passage is a bounteous corruption,
a dark voice drearing a tired lament.
You are a specter of old burlesque,
a shirtsleeved letch of clapping lust,
drooling the last song,
lost in a drifting dawn.
You are a morsel of entertainment
wasted by strangers,
a landless wanderer pleading arrivals,
eroding the book of enlightenment,
searching with wonder and anger
the land of visionless youth.

Distant Warning

May we never be called to judgment
for our deeds, or lack of deeds,
save by ourselves, beyond forgiveness,
sodden with toleration,
blind, with eyes that only see tomorrows,
that see our walled cities crumble,
that hear the piercing barbarian cries
as we yield our daughters to strangers.
We should see Rome around each corner,
a toothless lion squatting near the perch
of a molting eagle, rattling his epileptic claws.

Humanitas Rex

Tribal fires are mostly extinguished,
sending men to hulk in safer places.
Grunts and snarls become bewildered faces.
What replaces savagery relinquished?
War dances and auto-da-fes are departed.
The fear of night is hidden with inventions
that illuminate the world restarted,
shaped into acceptable conventions.
Marvel found by a remote and vanished (dare I say)
man, part ape, part hunger, one unflinching part
dreaming of glory, building the courage of day
from the terror of darkness that sets man apart
from other beasts as long as he believes,
smashing forever the limits of what he achieves
in the grandeur of endeavors whose only rival
is the miracle and arrogance of man's survival.

Dispossessed

Gently flows the night
in the fluttering city,
while a young sparrow
regains the nest.
Sinuously twines the night
around a supine city,
twisting serpentine coils,
choking, choking,
through the neon coldness,
on, off, on, off, until dawn.
Last weaver,
mad king of opiate visions,
blind captain tasting the fog
slinking past river midnights.
The heart pounds, stops,
pounds again.
Come home, come home,
dream ancient as the earth.

Thoughts of New York City

So many sirens proclaiming disasters,
fire, mugging, coronary, each
having its special colored truck,
rush urgent, but never enough
so we can close sleep eyes,
safe that the city will survive
too many threatening tomorrows.
Women assaulted on the streets
unprotected, undefended, unaided,
plead for help, then rely on self-defense,
tried as a felon
by the same court and judge
that suspends sentence on criminals.
The taxi drivers' barricades
that really convince no one
that they or you are safe,
for the jungle has entered the city
and tooth and claw click
as we measure each other,
disaster never far from desire
that law or myth must prevail.

Depot

The Port Authority Bus Terminal is not crowded at midnight. The night laborers going home to small houses in New Jersey, the servicemen displaced in their uniforms, returning to bases, the teenagers in couples, or in noisy herds, huddling together, bellowing about some glorious incident of the exciting evening in Sin City, the shabby loiterers, leftovers from another age, standing with hands in pockets, looking for tomorrows, and the eternal cripple of all public places, dragging a reluctant body to somewhere, blinded by yesterdays. They are the poem of the midnight bus depot of cities.

The shops of unfriendly storekeepers, swallowed by too many thousands in a hurry, are closed, along with their flowers, books, cigarettes, liquor, drugs, all to speed you on your way and ease you through another day. The huge rush-hour crowds are gone, with no sign of their passing, but gum-wrappers, cigarette butts, trash, left by what hand, what face, in this drab funnel to another place. The gravel-voices announcing departures in indifferent mumbles, directing to so many gates, people nowhere bound, blindly hoping to be found. Too warm, or too cold, walls too bare, a functional driveway of directions, and everywhere people untouched by loveliness, leaving no mark, or monument, pushing, sweating, arguing, farting, rushing, rushing, eyes closed to imaginings, except for frantic fantasies of sex, sleep, food, any detour from the starkness of this place, the midnight bus depot of cities.

Where do they go, the faceless thousands who step up to the ticket counter, pushing money through the slotted windows, mumbling a name to a tired clerk in shirtsleeves, pushing buttons on an aging machine that produces suddenly a ticket, to where? A thousand towns, villages and cities conjured to existence in this dark, consuming depot, by the restless fingers of a bored clerk. What do they do in the towns and cities? Are they returning home defeated by the great disinterest of the city, to remain, or lick their wounds and venture out again? Visiting family, friends, a school holiday, vacation, some loved-one's or unloved-one's funeral, a new job or home, a salesman conserving expenses, or someone drawn across this land by the strangeness and mystery of a name of a village, town, or city.

Inclusion

Young men should never spend days
dreaming old serenities,
remembering the past
interludes of strange contentment
when adrift in city passion,
hungering
fame,
women,
success,
while fingers of ambition
stroke soft, pale shoulders
and ice tinkles in thin-stemmed glasses,
sweaty on a Sutton Place terrace.
There is no rest from midnight lust
and late at night men lie abed
and cannot sleep
and sweat their sheets
and dream distant voyages
and find no protection from time.
Each day,
no nearer to fulfillment,
aging,
tiring,
learning fear,
becoming, at last,
like others.

Winter Night in Germany

There is no gradual decline of day
to prepare the people for evening.
The passing of the sun to grey
brooding skies is swift, without warning.
The shops are lit. Young, restless girls
fill orders and with anxious eyes watch snow
fall slowly on the streets in weary swirls
that soon are spun to ice and cast a dull glow.
The church bells sing loud. It is six thirty.
The lights wink out in offices and shops.
The trip home starts on never dirty
Strassenbahns, or orderly bus stops.
The evening meal is simple food, mostly cold
sausages, cheese, bread, and always beer
in huge amounts, for German stomachs hold
more than other stomachs and we always hear
the toasts: Prost, zum wohl.
Then lively stube or keller for more beer,
or the warmth of the cinema at eight,
visiting friends who welcome good cheer,
talk and drinking, but not leaving late.
Home again, quickly to bed,
almost everyone asleep by midnight.
All is still. The darkness men dread
remains until morning births its light.

South Bronx

In the dawn of cities
humans squat in crumbling houses
imprisoned by decay.
Predators possess the day,
destroyers rule the night.
Frightened families cling
to feeble, flickering hopes.
Tomorrow is a risky sleep away.
Some do not awaken,
while others learn survival.
Life is despair
when the world does not care.
As we forget the South Bronx,
hardly a ripple spreads
to trouble sleepers in protected beds.

Window View

Looking westward from my window
the sun leans backwards,
rushing towards Texas or Arizona,
leaving a delicate pink tint
on the tall buildings of Times Square.
The streets below fill and spill
with homeward bound, don't-look-around
workers, shoppers, tourists, seekers,
wanting peep shows, implements, drugs,
so many pausing for purchases, so many,
I did not know that vice possessed so many.
And wearily passing its filth to the sea,
once noble Hudson River, polluted and abused,
enduring man's assault, but weakening fast.
I see the spectacle of 42nd Street days,
the squalid nights of flesh-thrill hopes,
the kindless dawn with appetites unfulfilled,
leaving wanderers in a haze of dreams,
consigned to unachievements.

Victory

In a tiny room
sored with time-holes,
chipped paint, twists of dust,
curled asleep,
glob of dream child,
porter of tyrants.
Parents, friends, slum, school,
conspirators of vast burdens,
builders on pimpled shoulders.
Helot of eternal cities,
scabbed and scuffed,
will eye splendors,
barred for hungry fingers.
You are song,
sacrifice to drabness,
fragment of creation.
You must always be defeated,
tool of construction,
most sacred vessel.

Wanderer

Though I wander through my land
despised and shunned,
I never lived Long Island dreams,
wealthy and secure.
I wanted a Pacific sunset,
the mad-painted sky,
visionary cities.
I have lost the sunrise song
in the desert of nuclear waste,
the untrod path of inner fears,
subterranean desires
never spoken in the roadside pause.
The long, searing summer ache
sucking the juices from the land,
myself migratory,
a tongueless poet,
a churchless prophet.

La Passione

I hear your words
humming from a little mouth
unstopping.
You, me, fellow passengers,
subway denizens of a fiery land
with souls ablaze.

A shadow urchin pees on me.
Your station . . . Goodnight,
soggy girl of painted eyes.
A young boy eating cookies,
daddy floats on his balloon.
A worker asleep, at prayer,
fat slabs of chaffed fingers
clasped across an endless belly.
A Brooklyn gentleman,
neck erupting from Van Heusen shirt,
whose lower lip turns the pages
of *The New York Times* intensely.

I am no heir of kings,
painful in the chase of scalding dreams,
my days glow rich,
though sometime freighted
to a dark land of fruitless time,
but I will mend my Ozymandian fragments
and pursue the bright star that evades the dawn.

Journey

I have seen the bird of morning
and listened to its song,
while others passed unheeding.
I have watched man build his houses
on great streets and highways
and know I never want
the road snarl for my song.
As I caress you, dream city,
your spires of power and promise
hulk forbidding in the distance.
Your rigid face of stone and steel
indifferently turns away
from a bus of shabby hopes
bringing a seeker on his way.

Forlorn

She is not coming
and will never come again.
I will pass the many midnights
helpless as an amputee.
I shall not find
forgetfulness,
rehabilitation,
or opium stupefaction.
Existence shall continue
haphazard as crusades
and the dark Saracen will slash my armor
as I await the weary dawn
in pusillanimous imaginings.

Devourer

When the city almost sleeps,
when the last sentinels
of the vice-filled night
have grown hoarse
serenading passersby,
as the Times Square songs;
check it out, check it out,
loose joints, girls, girls,
become solo squalls
fading into hopes of morning,
there is a paralyzing hiss
as the serpent of squalor
feeds on men who do not sleep.
Bam. Crash. Clank . . .
The eater of the world has come,
announcing his ascension.

Hope

I have heard the rain hum evening
of my land's people
crying angry fears,
my land's people
raising a throbbing chant
surrendering our tomorrows.
Though come from once ship of trust,
fought hard and won,
stood tall over there,
in pride went far,
then faltered.
Not resolved
that conglomerates and cartels are continuations,
cycles always flexing shape and choice
and my people's land
is a young land,
learning to maintain the estate,
filling cities and forests with beginnings.
Growing
is my land's people.

Momentary Trace

Out of the lost passage of time
a schoolboy remembrance,
a face glimpsed in the city,
a passport to love and longing
that closed the doors of forgiveness,
denying the days of child apology,
when fault and sin could be forgotten,
while each tomorrow
exacts yesterday's error.

Doomed

Evenings of gentle touch linger
like the sex-sweet haunt of finger
gently stroking a lover's hair.
Past the waste bins of desire
the shadowed recollections of the liar
contract with audible despair.
We have walked the streets at dawn,
swallowed by the ravenous forgetting
of home and place and city,
where we live and have lived before,
by unused yesterdays devoured
of time, of face, or our passing
with sad detachment and bleak wonder,
fearing vision beyond confessing.
Uncertainty, ripped from bled imaginings,
while the graveyard tugs its ear and waits.

Crumbling City

The vision of a carven city,
hewn from alchemies of man's creation,
the sored members of imagination,
an old, voluptuous whore in decline.
On the once feudal streets,
coursing with refuse of pulsation,
bloated by this wearisome inflation,
the mechanic, foiled by spastic fingers.

Above the Fray

Faltering soul
on the East River terrace,
sad reflections dancing on the water
from corporate distractions,
Pan Am, Silvercup, Sunshine biscuits,
the monotony of cars passing,
the haunt-cry of tug-boat and dark barges . . .
Pharaoh's Nile never carried more dreams.
A distant auto horn, frightened,
a couple quarreling
under a thin, Sutton Place tree.
Inside, the party swirls,
the tedium of empty conversation
consumes ambition
like ravenous Pirana.

Unkind City

City of strangers, a patient trap
for vagrants on this earthly map,
opening gates and beckoning doors
for corrupters, scholars, thieves and bores,
enticing the evening with glittering sights
that conceal the refuse of squalid nights,
that strut by moonlight in arrogant display,
that ignores the horror that dawns each day.

Whether rocketing subway mobs uptown,
peeling soul like skin from summer fruit,
or having policemen club a derelict down,
the city is a mindless brute,
with little room for gentle faces.
Its arteries flow flint-hard men
carried to a hundred faddish places,
till fashion changes and they're off again.

And the people of the lavish shops
wrapped in greed, or envy's tears,
greet innocent desires with obscene leers
that beckon interchange, then stops.
The city should be closed to those with roots,
who seek to build a home and a family,
clutch with bitter dread for frail security,
that shatters, while the city jeers and hoots.

Fruitless Search

I kept a vigil,
driven from a thorny bed of sleep,
by ghostly visitant
who waved discoveries in gleaming hands.

Into the evening streets I rushed,
the calm, hazy sky and glistening lights
a seeming mockery of mysteries to come
on such a night of emanations.

I sought others,
hoping in the milling press to find
someone to share my neon appetite,
but nothing comes when sought in hunger.

How fast the streets were paced
by urgent, shuffling feet
fearing the brief expanse of night
would invite someone's fading.

Hours passed delivering the message,
unrevealed in fleeting motions.
No one left to meet in chance encounters,
no where left to go but home.

Nothing but another evening's desolation
gloating with many others,
leaving me marooned on lonely doorstep,
unconsoled by hints of dawn.

Tidal Sweep

Again in the silence of night
it is the woman who comes to me
for surrender until first light.
We met many dusks ago
and sojourned together,
until dawn drove her to the sea.
For she was a twilight lover,
compelled by mermaids of the morning
to clean the sands of lovers stains.

The Poet

Dreamer lost upon a narrow bed
watching with fear time pass away,
his feeble tongue leaves much unsaid
in wasted frenzy each fleeting day.
His thoughts are brooding, full of pity
fled to fantasies and sightless stare,
bewildered in a kindless city
cursing sadness, hating weak despair.
He cries defeat in battles yet unfought,
dreading the hour postponement fades,
alone in visions, and, in truth, unsought,
his failings strut in arrogant parades.
But day of growth and surge of power,
one song wrung from secret source,
and his poem constructs a soaring tower
where great beauty runs its course.

Survival Strain

Hastening birth to death,
dream city of dangerous dawns,
corpse of ceremonies
dropped from sooty womb,
nourished on cracked streets and crumbling subways,
nurtured by sirens and unanswered pleas for help.
Your sons and daughters are citizens of suspicion,
whose midnights have no more enchantment,
whose faces are birds of apprehension
singing no more songs of morning.

Inflamed

Night time in the South Bronx
conceals war-torn scars,
gaping wounds of crumbling homes,
abandonment, decay, despair
that consumes the rotting streets.
Only arson seems to care.
Light from houses, offices, cafés,
electrocutes people
caught in the wrong night,
possessed by flickering dreams
that ebb at the gift of dawn.

Effluvia

Before dawn
waves break loudest on beaches
when no one suns, or fumbles under blankets.
Morning light makes little whispers,
and horizons are attracted
to sand dune men
trudging the dank shore
seeking lost treasure.

Search

We walk the lonely streets of cities
lost to warmth and human roots,
peering in the storefront windows
at the excess of luxury,
staring at people bound for somewhere,
trapped in the anguish of the outcast,
shrinking from the judging eyes of strangers.
We shall walk the empty streets of cities
searching for the refuge of the moment,
the too-brief pause from crazed wandering
through the promise-world, yet undelivered,
hoping some tiny place upon the earth
will give us comfort and shelter,
before we are erased by dawn.

Fresh Air Camp

No mere sight of yellow flowers
opening in joyous showers
will quell the thought that quickly comes,
we must return to city slums.

No brief escape to pathless wood
that brings beauty we never could
hope to find at this guilty time,
when we atone for youthful crime.

We cannot make this forest stay
unchanged until another day,
when we escape poverty's lies
that imprison us, blind our eyes.

Winter City

The trees in front of shabby houses,
naked-armed like gangly urchins,
are snow-covered and aglitter.
People move cautiously on streets of ice,
sloshing through filthy puddles,
departing from the warmth of home.
They do not see the naked elegance
of one festive moment of winter,
thawing the coldest dawn.

Disenchantment

Each morning we arise
rushing to our known reality.
Marvels are spun
faster than dreams,
but forgotten as quickly,
upon awakening.
Tomorrow grows distant,
burdened by today.
Then go tongueless into city streets,
once proud, now whimpering for help,
past faces once scorned or mocked,
hungering the moment of a word.
Inhabitant of man's construction,
you may survive another dawn.

Varicose

Spring in the city so soon departed
that youthful glories must be boasted now,
when strength flows with furies undenied
by the sad settlements that age demands.

To wander rootless in this land,
an exile's bitter search,
denied remembrance of beginnings,
each face an unknown message,
lost in ancient hurts.

My tongue not a bird-cry moment
high flown from cloud fingers,
but a helpless fleck of yearnings
adrift in city stillness,
crumbling from the loss of purpose,
a distant shadow of misadventure.

Faded Fabric

In the dark longings of the night, on streets where hushed voices are channeled by unyielding portals, men peer down shadowy alleys and hope to find in one desperate, all-embracing glance, the root of life. I have heard voices in the night and they have cried their siren-call to the core of my heart. I have passed strangers walking in the night and my tongue has almost poured out my yearnings, as their backs passed into darkness. I have listened to the great silence that falls in the dim passages before dawn and I have known that we must sometimes rest. I have seen your bright lights that cast beaconed shafts throughout the night that never dies. And I have been haunted by the active ghost of the pulsing city, which sends out throbbing waves, denying release, that bear the hue of the grey dwellers of the city.

Recurrence

It is the twilight hour of silence.
The slumberous streets are empty
save for the walkers until sunrise
who haunt the paved lanes
awaiting the dawn of tomorrow,
which comes in opaque, orange gleams,
revealing filth abandoned
by the resentful death of yesterday.

Isolani

It is the hour of the sparrow at sunset.
Throughout the falling silent streets
an evening peace descends.
Home to the hearth go the spirits of labor,
awaited by tender women
and happy children.
But those who go into the twilight,
alone in a world of pained revery,
know no comfort.
They are the walkers of solitary streets
from sunset to the trembling dawn
thirsting for fulfillment,
watching mournful rivers flow,
yearning for the wisdom of the wind,
dreading the spirit of the night.

Rent Due

Knowing you are not an echo
and only extended convalescence
will heal the emasculate breach in me,
I cry farewell, across city canyons.
But you, too busy tourist,
bend one abortive knee
before your clutching whim,
and never pause to listen
to my solitary song
that creeps past dawn
to the garbage copse of tenements,
until it's swallowed by the East River.

Weary Road

I have traveled far,
a rootless wanderer
singing the praises of man,
mouthing the phrases of fools.
Ruled by the hand of dawn,
city, your shadows are silence
that lead me to desolate roads,
with no end to journeys.
At night the stars surrender
to your shattering glare, city,
that winks in flirting allure
and urges me on to Babylon.

Release

The night yowl
of the alley cat,
with the earthly burden
of nine lives,
rends the silent air,
awakening the slumbering corpses
from infinite reveries,
in soporific dreams
of earth madness
that were fettered
by the bonds of sleep.

Settlement

City caravan of strangers
who have permanently halted,
twined together in uncertainty
and planted buildings of survival
possessed by expectations
of safety from nomads,
you have lost purpose
in walls of entombment.

Encounter

How can I sing
of the tired, old Jewish man
of subway mornings
and strange remembrance,
spawned in some distant ghetto,
bearing the scar of lost roots,
still tortured by Cossack dreams?
I look up from my naval,
see your face of prayers,
holier than death,
or are you death,
wearing a sad dreamer's cloak?
Old man of unequality,
hornless, unterrible,
you must have a wife,
more ancient monkey of sorrow
than woman.
Evening after work
you listen to violin music
on your console radio.
O leaf blown through
this strange world,
I'll look for you tomorrow.

Renewal

Rushing footsteps poke the light from hiding.
Morning faces shaven, or new-painted,
peek behind yawns at wristwatches,
as engines belch from parking places.
The winter darkness stretches its toes,
departing with reluctance as shops open.
Fresh bread snuggles on the shelves,
rubbing tantalizing odors on dawn-smudged windows
as we renew our hunger for the hope of day
and continue the rite of existence.

Foreign Dream

Stirring slow or faster in the night,
dread silence, found in sleeping cities
where virgins shyly dance before their mirrors,
nur ohne licht,
turning to intense inspections, soft
as murmurs passing windows, briefly heard
from strangers never seen, somewhere bound,
der Fluss fliest,
pausing only for reflections on a mighty bridge,
light, gauze yellow or unholy white, bursting
into calmness, when ships cease disturbance.
Herst du mich?
From motions of crossings in the final journey, nothing
halts. But stirrings slow or faster, move
in unfelt currents, changes, untouched by dawn.
Diese zeit, fremd.

Intermezzo

The shrieks of children
pierce the rumble-roar of city streets.
Just this once the cries don't mean
threat, crime, terror, pain,
just the exuberant delight
for those brief moments
of playful youth.

Frail Victims

The whine faces of the city
never find pity
looking to others,
who are implosion men,
quick to profit now and then,
from another's frailness.
The desperation streets collapse
beneath a milligram of tears,
dropped from eyes of silent fears,
that in the moment of confrontation,
succumb to urban abomination.

Revels Ended

We have dreamed your spires and towers, city,
raised you not quite cloud-high,
bursted your innards with commotion,
threatened with dreadful intention,
bringing fear to your people,
filling the streets with terror.
We have betrayed the covenant of tomorrow,
consuming today with material pleasures.

Confusion

Midnight wanderings
in the sleepless city
lead to dawn awakenings.
Hints of spring slip up the nostrils
breeding drowsy imaginings.
Does the world ever nap?
We are restless, rootless . . .
Adrift in urban dream
that nightmares our expectations.

Downward Spiral

Voracious cities of decay
that spread across our tortured land,
extending encrusted arms
with slum-tainted fingers
that strain to touch each other
with the multiflavored, democratic rot
that breeds in urban American places.

Survival

City cat, bloated with young,
belly lower than legs,
steps into the light . . .
God it's tiny . . .
Statutory rape,
kitten had by brutal tom.
I fetch canned salmon,
cater an unexpected feast.
Bulging, famished mama
nibbles daintily,
eyes turn like periscope
scanning hostile shores.
Finishes. Washes.
Slinks under rusting car,
resuming journeys.
Tired of wandering,
dawn seeks its bed.

Emergency

The buildings rise in angry bruises,
beaten by night's thin skin.
The city's desperate cry for help
is throttled by TV antennas.
The air dribbles old men stuff
that stains and smears our visions.
The siren of forgiveness sounds
the last attention to tomorrow.

Burden

When midnight visions pass us on the street,
opera, party, other brief retreat
that should bring awe, like old biblical men
in a visit that heralds promise, then,
a puzzled shaking of a skeptics head,
lose sight and slink home to poverty bed.

Sightless

The reflection of light
through tainted air,
etches the moment
on gloating buildings,
blinding people
and drowns the stars,
until the dawn
annuls our vision.

Dwindling Times

The gates of cities have fallen
and battle is technic and unshining.
We are a somber, democratic age
that has placed glory in storage—
but slaughter fifty years removed
still awakens bold remembrance—
an ancient rite revived
only for the chosen son
of the suffering republic
in need of heroes.

Formula

There are dreams that you and I can share,
but it is a tenuous construction,
built of ether, water, earth and air,
a resurrection or destruction.
Something passed between us
like a lost legend in the night,
something startled and ambiguous
flicked into view, then leaped out of sight.

Dancing a dawn of hovering love,
whispering between crisp sheets,
elevating us far above
sinuous windings of tenement streets.
I see it glaring from an urchin's eyes,
dribbling from a beggar's lips,
falling from chemical skies
upon your succulent hips.

Boycott

The boys of the Bronx
often never learn
they've been abandoned,
until too late
to rebuild the lost youth
that leads to confidence.
So many Bronx boys
judged and found worthless,
condemned for dark skin,
different accent,
whose neglectful parents
have been found wanting
for not providing
alligator shirts,
passports to privilege
that open the portals
to life's purchased pleasures.

Harsh Clime

Unkind citadel attracting strangers
searching for the elusive dream,
confronted by your pitiless face,
glass, metal, stone, wood,
all decaying features
of your jagged smile, city,
enduring no plot for refuge.
Disarming fortress of surrender,
your terror corrupts the citizens
not reconciled to your injustice.

Refuge

Into the mad soliloquy of cities,
finding no relief in escape,
books, drinks, drugs, flesh,
unavoidable delusions.
Fearful as some harried prey
followed by a relentless hunter,
we are desperate to rest
and gather warrior strength,
but our hands don't hold stout spears
and we do not find battle's resolution,
just the endless combat,
merciless and sly,
with the undefeatable craven,
our shirking selves.

Grim Urb

Pale sun of winter city,
consuming us,
with your distant grin
from frigid buildings
that lick the damp sky,
implacable as old men,
sucking the heat after dawn.

Last Ride

Throughout your streets of filth
the gritty children
roam unexplored paths
of everyday horror,
taking this man's curse,
that man's foot,
until they go home
to mother's piercing shriek,
father's furious fists.
Tomorrow comes
with spatial flights of fancy,
upon your horse,
or in your spaceship,
away you go
to far horizons,
until the screech of brakes,
the jarring thud,
ends your ride.

Tread Lightly

Intangible wilderness
that sometimes possesses us
in the myth of civilization,
is all that holds
this raptured city from destruction.
Do the poets who sing of the city
know anything of the city?
When we are the only core
that keeps reality together,
for surely if our reasoning selves
suddenly were to doubt
that our subway days
and rummage-sale nights
were all the glory
we ever would obtain,
in that faithless moment,
nature, in her new sneakers,
would place her arch-supported,
space-age ventilated soles,
on eight million delusions
and pffffft . . .

Rebirth

We have lurched and fallen
in our long journey
through the flesh of cities,
crazed by lust,
blinded by fear,
crushing soft bodies
mad with drugs and drink,
until an angel's appearance
greeted the bright dawn,
promising salvation.

Nomad

I fall upon the world of promise
a hungry Goth, or Vandal,
battering on Roman doors.
I am soothed by pledges
and pause assaults
in expectation of a triumph.
Seduced by city ways,
I ponder the changes
from shabby cloth
to splendid garments,
then the chilling voice of dawn
drives me to migrations.

Luminous

The lights of cars, trucks, buses
pierce the dark streets of night,
birthing us brief kin a moment,
as we race past unknown places,
hastening to the dawn of the city
that would dispossess us.

Lily

Lily Carver,
who had great legs
for a young girl
and a hard to resist mouth
for young boys,
despite her mothers urgent cries,
would go late at night
behind the fence in the schoolyard
and collect coins from strangers,
until dawn drove her to bed.

Last Chance

Our tomorrow may perish
while we, sinned against, or sinning,
sleep our fleeting days away.
This sorriest creation clot,
blighted city,
where we whimper longings,
yet consume the future
in bloated feastings
couched and dreamy,
lost in expectations
that make us wait and wait and wait,
until our moment fades.

Detached

Among our fevered expectations
there is no time for interruption,
when the meetings of strangers
break forth into praises.
City, your men who tread grit-streets
are fugitives from combustible places,
trapped in summer climes, with unthawed faces
that no longer seek the dawn's arising,
who dwell in awkward hesitations,
by the measures of distance
from sheltered places
abandoned in the wasted siege
that shore no longer seen.

City Dump

Renovate your treasure room,
or waste will insure our doom.
Metal, garbage, gas and hair,
cast upon our rivers where
returned tenfold to add to blight
that withers visions of our light.

Age

The refusing to be old
women of bleached hair
and too-tight dresses
walk the unkind summer streets,
whose bright lights
and windows of reflection
begin each dawn.
They always wear sunglasses,
pointy shoes and flashy colors,
seeking concealment from aging.
Too fleshed and too tanned,
they pout time's passing.

Across the River

Brooklyn, a separation
from the illusion of the city,
almost a forgotten place,
despite great bridges and parks,
marred by too many drab buildings,
on miles of residential streets,
where garbage decorates the trees,
bicycle wheel dangling on a rotting branch,
old sneakers, plastic bags, detritus.
This place of night silence,
where workers fall into their beds
earlier than in other cities,
a journey through devouring cells.
Not many strangers pass
in the darkness of your streets.
Oh lost and fading land,
peopled by phantoms
so quickly gone,
that give not comfort.

An Altar

This almost city
gasping,
a frail bandit
stealing
whatever hope breeds.
Peopleless and poor
the mythic strollers
are not ethereal in search
and in the sun,
hot and pregnant,
before the portals of Macy's
they kindle drab secrets
and leer genuflections.

Progress

The light of dawn
falls upon the works of man,
whose bridges, builder,
have no time to topple.
Across the great divide
of cities in conflict,
your wonderous structures
span the dying waters,
pass through poisoned air,
assaulted by men
moved by steel and wheel
faster to escape the fumes of guilt,
who neglect tomorrows
for tonight's late entertainment,
an ellipse of reason,
from which we may not emerge.

About the Author

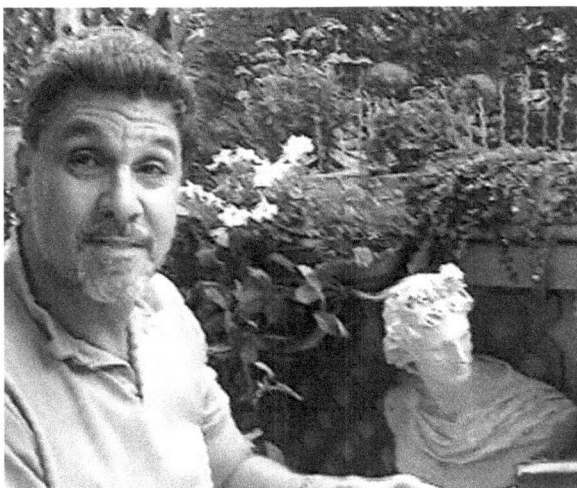

Gary Beck has spent most of his adult life as a theater director. He has had numerous published works including *Days of Destruction* and *Expectations*. His novel, *Extreme Change*, was published by Cogwheel Press. Gary has also had several original plays and translations produced off Broadway, in New York City where he currently resides.

Find out more about Gary on his website: GaryCBeck.com

www.ingramcontent.com/pod-product-compliance
Lightning Source LLC
Chambersburg PA
CBHW071503070426
42452CB00041B/2275